The Complete Cookie Cookbook For Beginners

365 Days Of Delicious And Affordable Recipes To Break Free From Culinary Routine And Delight Your Family On Every Occasion

By
Rosy Mckenney

Table of Contents

Introduction

Cookies are beloved in kitchens and hearts worldwide. They provide a pleasant taste and sweetness that transcends countries and generations. Cookies provide delight and comfort, whether eaten with milk before bed or as a special treat. We'll explore cookies' history, role in current times, and the fun of preparing them in your own home.

The Historical Origin of Cookies

Cookie origins span millennia and are as varied as the cookies we enjoy today. Although determining when cookies were invented is difficult, we may trace their history across many cultures and historical periods.

One of the first biscuits was made in 7th-century Persia. Early cookies, called "cakies," included water, sugar, and fat. Explorers and warriors loved them because of their mobility and shelf life. Cookies developed and spread worldwide. Small, spiced biscuits were popular in Europe, especially during the Middle Ages. These were often given as presents and goodwill during holidays.

Cookies were created in the American colonies during the 17th century owing to

European immigrants. Local resources like molasses and cornmeal were used in early American cookies. They symbolized hospitality when served with tea or coffee.

By the 20th century, cookies were a household staple. Toll House invented the chocolate chip cookie, establishing its position in American society. Traditional traditions from many civilizations mixed, creating an amazing variety of cookie tastes, textures, and forms.

Cookies in Modern Times

Cookies have grown from modest origins to worldwide phenomenon. They are in bakeries, supermarkets, and kitchens worldwide. Versatility makes cookies beautiful. Everyone can enjoy a chewy chocolate chip cookie, delicate shortbread, or spicy ginger snap.

Cookie making has revived in the digital era. Online forums and culinary blogs make sharing cookie recipes, ideas, and methods easy. Social media is full with delicious handmade cookie photos, tempting bakers of all abilities to try their own.

Healthy and dietary-specific cookies are in demand. To accommodate different diets, bakeries are using almond flour, coconut oil, and natural sweeteners. Gluten-free, vegan, and keto-friendly cookies are now accessible, indicating that cookies may satisfy health-conscious customers without sacrificing flavor.

Discovering the Joy of Baking

The process of preparing cookies is fun for many, not the finished result. Baking cookies is a simple yet rewarding way to bring pleasure to your home.

Choose a recipe that suits your tastes and imagination. The choices are unlimited whether you want classics or novel flavors. Mixing the ingredients, feeling the dough come together, and shaping it into tasty treats may be relaxing.

Your house smells like cookies, building anticipation. Golden-brown cookies fresh from the oven are amazing. The finest part is enjoying your creation. That first mouthful, frequently warm from the oven, is sheer joy.

Cookie baking may be a single hobby, family enjoyment, or buddy activity. Sharing baked cookies with family produces lasting memories. Let's promote joy, love, and cherish life's wonderful moments.

We want to capture cookies' history, relevance, and delight in this cookbook. This book has something for every baker, from beginners to experts. So grab your apron, preheat the oven, and explore the world of cookies. A voyage of history, invention, and, most importantly, baking delight.

Chapter 1:
Mastering the Basics of Cookie Baking

Baking cookies is easy and fun, but there is a science behind it that may improve your abilities. This chapter will explore the art and science of making cookies and the fundamentals that make a great batch. The chemistry of cookies, the foundational components, and the baking procedures that create or break them will be covered. You'll understand what makes a cookie great at the conclusion of this chapter.

The Science of Baking Cookies

Fundamentally, baking may be seen as a scientific discipline. Gaining a comprehensive comprehension of the scientific principles behind the production of cookies not only facilitates the consistent achievement of delectable outcomes but also enables effective problem-solving in instances of unexpected deviations from the intended outcome.

Basic cookies include butter, sugar, flour, and leavening ingredients like baking soda or baking powder. When these components are mixed, complex chemical reactions occur during baking, creating delicious textures, tastes, and scents.

The Maillard reaction is a fundamental chemical process that plays a crucial role in the production of cookies. The aforementioned procedure entails the Maillard reaction, which encompasses the non-enzymatic browning of sugars and amino acids under the influence of thermal energy. The golden-brown hue and flavorful essence of cookies may be attributed to this particular component. A comprehensive comprehension of the temporal and procedural aspects involved in attaining the Maillard reaction is crucial for attaining optimal results in the Pre of cookies.

Temperature control is another crucial aspect of cookie baking science. Accurate oven temperature, along with the use of timers, can significantly impact the final result. Oven temperature affects how cookies spread, rise, and ultimately achieve their texture. Investing in an oven thermometer is a simple yet effective way to ensure your cookies bake at the right temperature.

Key Ingredients for Perfect Cookies

Every cookie recipe begins with a set of core ingredients, each playing a specific role in the final product. Let's take a closer look at these essential components:

- **Butter:** Butter adds flavor, moisture, and richness to cookies. Its fat content creates a tender texture, while its water content generates steam during baking, contributing to a light and airy structure.
- **Sugar:** Sugar provides sweetness and caramelization. It not only sweetens the cookies but also helps with browning and contributes to their chewiness or crispiness, depending on the type and quantity used.
- **Flour:** Flour gives cookies structure. The type of flour and its protein content affect the cookie's texture. More protein leads to a chewier cookie, while less protein results in a more delicate, tender texture.
- **Leavening Agents:** Baking soda and baking powder are leavening agents that help cookies rise. Baking soda requires an acidic ingredient (like brown sugar or buttermilk) to activate, producing carbon dioxide gas for lift. Baking powder contains both an acid and a base and can provide leavening without additional acidic ingredients.

Understanding the role of these ingredients and their interactions can help you adjust and customize your cookie recipes to achieve your desired taste and texture.

Essential Baking Techniques

Baking techniques play a crucial role in the success of your cookies. Here are some fundamental techniques to master:

- **Measuring Ingredients:** Accuracy in measuring ingredients is essential. Use dry measuring cups for dry ingredients like flour and sugar, and liquid measuring cups for wet ingredients like vanilla extract and milk.

- **Creaming Butter and Sugar:** Creaming butter and sugar together is a crucial step in cookie baking. It incorporates air into the mixture, leading to a lighter texture. Be sure to cream until the mixture is light and fluffy.
- **Mixing Dry and Wet Ingredients:** Combine dry and wet ingredients just until they are incorporated. Overmixing can lead to tough cookies.
- **Chilling Dough**: Many cookie recipes benefit from chilling the dough before baking. This helps solidify the fats in the dough, resulting in less spreading during baking and a thicker, chewier texture.
- **Proper Cookie Spacing:** Leave enough space between cookies on the baking sheet to allow for spreading during baking.

You'll be well on your way to being a competent and self-assured cookie baker if you familiarize yourself with the science behind cookie baking, become an expert with the important ingredients, and practice the fundamental skills. With enough experience, you'll be able to modify and develop cookie recipes that are uniquely suited to your preferences and sense of flavor. Baking success to you!

Chapter 2:
Exploring Dough Styles and Techniques

In the realm of cookie baking, possessing knowledge about the many types of cookie dough and the corresponding methodologies may significantly impact the ultimate outcome. The result of your baked goods, whether they are soft and chewy, crisp and delicate, or somewhere in between, is contingent upon your selection of dough style and the manner in which you manipulate it. This section will explore several forms of cookie dough, provide recommendations for choosing the most suitable one to achieve desired outcomes, and provide crucial methods for achieving successful cookie baking.

Styles of Cookie Dough

1. Drop Cookie Dough

Definition: Drop cookie dough is one of the most common and beginner-friendly styles.

Characteristics: They are known for their rustic appearance and irregular shapes.

Best Suited For: versatile and can accommodate a wide range of mix-ins, from nuts to chocolate chunks.

2. Sandy Cookie Dough

Definition: Sandy cookie dough, also known as shortbread dough, results in delicate and crumbly cookies. It's characterized by a high butter-to-flour ratio.

Characteristics: Sandy cookies are tender and melt in your mouth. They are not overly sweet and often feature a rich buttery flavor.

Best Suited For: Shortbread cookies, a prime example of sandy cookie dough, are wonderful on their own or as a base for various flavors and add-ins like lemon zest, lavender, or chocolate drizzle.

3. Roll-Out Cookie Dough

Definition: Roll-out cookie dough, sometimes referred to as sugar cookie dough, is designed for rolling and cutting into shapes. It holds its form well during baking.

Characteristics: Roll-out cookies are sturdy and maintain their shapes, making them ideal for intricate designs and decorating with icing or fondant.

Best Suited For: Holiday and special occasion cookies that demand precise shapes and decorations, such as gingerbread men, Christmas trees, and heart-shaped cookies for Valentine's Day.

4. Bar Cookie Dough

Definition: Bar cookie dough is pressed or spread into a pan, then baked and cut into squares or bars once cooled. It simplifies the process of making multiple cookies at once.

Characteristics: Bar cookies can vary widely in texture, from soft and fudgy (as in brownies) to crumbly and dense (like shortbread bars).

Best Suited For: Bar cookie dough is excellent for time-saving treats like brownies, blondies, and lemon bars. They're perfect for potlucks and picnics.

Choosing the Right Dough

The careful selection of the appropriate dough type is of utmost importance in order to get the intended texture and taste throughout the process of embarking on a cookie-making endeavor. There are many variables that should be taken into consideration before making a decision:

Chapter 3:
Stocking Your Cookie Pantry

The act of baking cookies has both artistic and scientific elements. In order to carry out experiments effectively, it is important for a scientist to possess the appropriate components. A pantry that is adequately supplied with essential ingredients serves as the fundamental basis for engaging in the activity of cookie making, therefore guaranteeing the availability of all necessary items anytime one is inclined to engage in this culinary pursuit. This part will delve into the fundamental components that are need, the gradual development of your baking pantry, and the modification of recipes using alternative products to accommodate personal tastes or dietary limitations.

Must-Have Baking Ingredients

Every baker, whether novice or seasoned, needs a set of foundational ingredients that serve as the building blocks for countless cookie recipes. These ingredients are the workhorses of your pantry, and having them readily available ensures you can whip up cookies at a moment's notice.

1. **All-Purpose Flour:** This is the backbone of most cookie recipes. It provides structure and texture to your cookies.
2. **Granulated Sugar:** Sugar not only sweetens your cookies but also contributes to their texture, tenderness, and color.

3. **Brown Sugar:** Both light and dark brown sugars add moisture, flavor, and a delightful caramel note to your cookies.
4. **Butter:** Unsalted butter is the go-to fat for cookies, providing richness and flavor. Make sure it's at room temperature for easy incorporation.
5. **Eggs:** Eggs act as binders and provide structure and moisture to your cookies. Always have a few in the fridge.
6. **Baking Soda and Baking Powder:** These leavening agents are essential for creating the right cookie rise and texture. Check their expiration dates regularly.
7. **Vanilla Extract:** A splash of pure vanilla extract enhances the flavor of your cookies, giving them a warm and inviting aroma.
8. **Salt:** Salt enhances flavor, balances sweetness, and brings out the nuances in your cookies. Use kosher or sea salt for best results.
9. **Chocolate Chips or Chunks:** Whether you prefer semisweet, dark, or white chocolate, having a stash of chocolate chips or chunks opens up a world of cookie possibilities.
10. **Nuts:** Almonds, walnuts, pecans, or other nuts of your choice can add texture and flavor to your cookies.
11. **Flavorings and Extracts:** Beyond vanilla, consider other extracts like almond, lemon, or peppermint to infuse unique flavors into your cookies.

Building Your Pantry

The process of establishing a comprehensive baking pantry needs a considerable amount of time, hence it is advisable to refrain from hastily procuring all the necessary items in a single instance. In order to establish a varied and well-stocked pantry, it is advisable to progressively amass the aforementioned things.

1. **Flour Varieties:** Experiment with different flours like whole wheat, pastry flour, or cake flour for unique cookie textures.
2. **Sugars:** Explore specialty sugars like powdered sugar, confectioners' sugar, and even coconut sugar for various flavor profiles.
3. **Spices and Herbs**: Cinnamon, nutmeg, ginger, and cardamom are spices known for their capacity to augment the taste characteristics of cookies, contributing to a heightened feeling of intricacy and a pleasurable perception of warmth.
4. **Dried Fruits:** Raisins, cranberries, apricots, and cherries are excellent add-ins for cookies, providing bursts of sweetness and chewiness.
5. **Citrus Zest:** Lemon, orange, or lime zest can brighten up the flavor of your cookies.
6. **Extracts and Emulsions:** Branch out with flavors like maple, coconut, or coffee extracts for unique cookie experiences.
7. **Gluten-Free Flours:** In the event that an individual or their close associates possess dietary limitations, it is advisable to get an ample supply of gluten-free flours such

as almond flour, rice flour, or coconut flour.
8. **Alternative Sweeteners:** Experiment with honey, maple syrup, or agave nectar as sugar substitutes in your cookie recipes.
9. **Plant-Based Ingredients:** If you're baking for vegans, have non-dairy milk, flaxseeds, or aquafaba (chickpea brine) on hand as egg replacements.
10. **Specialty Chocolate:** Dive into the world of high-quality chocolates with cocoa powder, chocolate bars, or cocoa nibs for gourmet cookies.

Adapting with Alternative Ingredients

On some occasions, individuals may find it necessary to modify a cookie recipe in order to accommodate particular tastes or dietary requirements. Presented below are many practical suggestions for replacing components in cookie recipes:

- **Butter Alternatives:** Coconut oil, applesauce, or mashed bananas can replace butter for a dairy-free option.
- **Egg Replacements:** Try silken tofu, yogurt, or a commercial egg replacer for vegan or egg-free cookies.
- **Gluten-Free Flours:** Cookies made without the presence of gluten may be crafted using ingredients such as almond flour, oat flour, or a gluten-free flour mix.
- **Sugar Substitutes:** Stevia, erythritol, or xylitol can replace sugar for low-sugar or sugar-free cookies.
- **Nuts and Allergies:** If allergies are a concern, experiment with seed butters (e.g., almond butter), sunflower seeds, or coconut flakes as alternatives to nuts.
- **Dietary Preferences:** Adjust spices, extracts, and sweeteners to cater to dietary preferences, creating cookies that are keto, paleo, or low-carb.

In summary, having a well equipped pantry serves as a valuable asset in the pursuit of crafting delectable cookies. Commence with acquiring the essential components, progressively extend your assortment, and show willingness to explore substitute items in order to accommodate personal preferences or dietary requirements. Equipped with a diverse array of ingredients at your disposal, you are prepared to begin upon a novel and exciting endeavor in the realm of cookie-baking. Engage in the joyful act of baking!

Chapter 4:
Decorating Cookies Like a Pro

The act of embellishing cookies has the potential to elevate a basic assortment of baked confections into a masterpiece. The acquisition of cookie decorating skills may provide great satisfaction, whether one is engaged in baking for a significant event, a festive occasion, or just for personal enjoyment. This chapter aims to examine various creative ways, go into the realm of frosting and chocolate, and uncover presentation ideas that might elevate the prominence of your cookies.

Creating Decorating Techniques

The act of decorating cookies provides individuals with the opportunity to showcase their artistic abilities and imbue their baked products with a distinctive and unique flair. In this discourse, we will examine a range of methodologies that have the potential to enhance one's proficiency in the art of cookie decoration.

Painting with Food Coloring

Food coloring can be a painter's best friend when it comes to cookies. You can create intricate designs, watercolor effects, or simply add vibrant hues to your cookies. Start by using food coloring gel or paste, which provides more concentrated and vivid colors than liquid food coloring. Mix your colors on a palette, and use fine paintbrushes to apply your edible paint to your cookies. This technique is perfect for creating detailed designs, such as flowers, animals, or abstract patterns.

Piping and Flooding with Royal Icing

Royal icing is a versatile medium that can be used to pipe intricate designs onto cookies. Piping involves outlining your design with a thicker consistency icing, while flooding involves filling in the outlined areas with a thinner consistency icing. With practice, you can create beautiful, professional-looking designs on your cookies. Invest in piping tips and bags, and experiment with different nozzle shapes to achieve different effects.

Texture with Stencils

Stencils provide a convenient method for incorporating texture and elaborate designs into biscuits. The use of pre-existing stencils or the creation of personalized designs are both viable options. To get a traditional aesthetic, affix the stencil firmly into the surface of the cookie, and afterwards apply a layer of powdered sugar or cocoa powder. In addition, one may choose to use royal icing or airbrushing techniques as alternative methods to produce intricate and vibrant patterns. Stencils prove to be particularly advantageous in the creation of themed cookies for various festivals and holidays.

Icing, Chocolate, and Sprinkles

Icing, chocolate, and sprinkles are the fundamental building blocks of cookie decoration. Let's explore how you can use these elements to enhance the appearance and taste of your cookies.

Royal Icing: The Ultimate Cookie Canvas

Its smooth texture and ability to harden make it ideal for creating detailed designs, from delicate lace patterns to intricate flowers. To achieve different consistencies (outline, flood, and detail), you can adjust the amount of water in your icing. For a glossy finish, add a touch of corn syrup. Royal icing can be tinted with food coloring to achieve a wide range of shades.

Chocolate: A Tempering Art

Chocolate offers a delicious and visually appealing way to decorate cookies. Melting and tempering chocolate can be a bit tricky, but it's worth the effort. Once properly tempered, chocolate will set with a beautiful shine and satisfying snap. Use a parchment paper cone or a piping bag to drizzle or pipe chocolate designs onto your cookies. You can also dip cookies into melted chocolate for a luxurious coating. Dark, milk, and white chocolates each bring their unique flavor profiles to your cookies, allowing for endless creative possibilities.

Sprinkles: A Splash of Color and Texture

The use of sprinkles is a convenient method for incorporating vibrant hues and varied tactile sensations into one's cookies. They exhibit a wide range of forms, sizes, and colors, making them appropriate for diverse events. Sprinkle the confectionery toppings over the just frosted cookies, and delicately apply pressure to promote adhesion. Themed sprinkles may be used to align with the intended purpose of the cookie, such as heart-shaped sprinkles for Valentine's Day or pumpkin-shaped sprinkles for Halloween. It is important to note that in the context of sprinkles, a greater quantity is often seen as more desirable.

Elevate Your Cookie Experience with Perfect Pairings

Pairing cookies with various beverages is a delightful journey that can elevate your cookie experience to new heights. The art of selecting the right drink to complement your favorite cookies enhances the flavors, textures, and overall enjoyment of your sweet treats. From classic combinations like milk and chocolate chip cookies to more creative pairings, there are endless possibilities to explore.

1. Milk and Chocolate Chip Cookies:

Chocolate chips are sweet and sticky, while milk is chilled and creamy. If you choose full, skim, or almond milk, the outcome is a pleasant taste and texture combination great for dipping cookies.

2. Tea and Shortbread Cookies:

Pairing delicate shortbread cookies with a cup of tea is a match made in cookie heaven. The subtle, buttery sweetness of shortbread beautifully complements the soothing, aromatic qualities of tea. You can opt for black tea, green tea, herbal tea, or even a classic English breakfast tea, depending on your preference. The slight bitterness of the tea works wonders with the buttery richness of shortbread, creating a refined and elegant combination.

3. Coffee and Rich, Chewy Cookies:

Strong coffee and thick, chewy biscuits are a fantastic pairing for coffee aficionados. The powerful tastes of espresso, dark roast, or latte enhance cookies' rich, chewy texture. Deep-flavored sweets like double chocolate or espresso-infused cookies match well with this combo. The harshness of coffee and the sweetness of cookies create a delicious taste balance.

4. Hot Chocolate and Marshmallow-Topped Cookies:

If you're a fan of hot chocolate, pairing it with marshmallow-topped cookies can take your winter indulgence to the next level. The warmth and creaminess of hot chocolate combined with the gooey marshmallow topping on your cookies create a cozy, comforting experience. This pairing is like a hug in a mug, especially on a cold winter's day.

5. Fruit Tea and Citrus-Flavored Cookies:

For a refreshing and zesty pairing, consider enjoying citrus-flavored cookies with fruit tea. The bright and tangy notes in citrus cookies, such as lemon or orange, complement the fruity flavors in fruit tea. The combination is a burst of sunshine in your mouth, making it an excellent choice for a light and invigorating snack.

6. Sparkling Water and Light, Crispy Cookies:

For those seeking a more refreshing and health-conscious option, pair sparkling water with light, crispy cookies like biscotti or meringue cookies. The effervescence of the sparkling water cleanses your palate between each bite of the airy, crispy cookies. This pairing is not only delicious but also a guilt-free indulgence.

7. Red Wine and Dark Chocolate Cookies:

For an adult treat, consider red wine with dark chocolate biscuits. Red wine's diverse flavors—red berries, oak, and spices—balance dark chocolate biscuits' bittersweet taste. This classy combo is excellent for a relaxing evening or special event.

In conclusion, the world of cookie and beverage pairings offers a wide range of choices to suit different tastes and moods. Whether you prefer the classic comfort of milk and cookies or enjoy experimenting with unique combinations, there's a perfect pairing waiting to be discovered. So, the next time you indulge in your favorite cookies, don't forget to consider the perfect beverage to accompany them – it's a culinary adventure worth exploring.

Presentation Ideas

The presentation of your cookies can be just as important as their taste and decoration. Here are some ideas to make your cookies look as good as they taste:

Gift-Worthy Packaging

When gifting cookies, presentation is key. Consider packaging your cookies in decorative boxes, bags, or jars. Personalize the packaging with labels, ribbons, or handwritten notes to make your cookies feel extra special. A beautifully wrapped batch of cookies can brighten anyone's day.

Cookie Bouquets

Turn your cookies into a stunning edible arrangement by attaching them to sticks or straws and arranging them in a vase or container. You can create cookie bouquets for birthdays, weddings, or any special occasion. It's a unique way to showcase your decorating skills and make a memorable gift.

Cookie Platters and Displays

For gatherings and parties, arrange your decorated cookies on a platter or display board. Consider creating a thematic arrangement, such as a cookie cake or a cookie wreath, to serve as a centerpiece. These eye-catching displays will entice your guests and add a touch of elegance to your event.

Cookie Decorating Stations

Set up a cookie decorating station at your events or gatherings. Provide plain, freshly baked cookies and an array of colorful icings, sprinkles, and toppings. Allow guests to unleash their creativity and decorate their own cookies. It's a fun and interactive way to entertain your guests and create delicious, custom treats.

Cookie Sliders

Create cookie sliders by sandwiching your cookies with delectable fillings like ice cream, whipped cream, or ganache. This innovative presentation adds an element of surprise and indulgence to your cookies, making them perfect for dessert time. Serve them with a variety of fillings and let your guests customize their cookie sliders to their liking.

Cookie Jar Centerpieces

Transform cookie jars into elegant centerpieces for your dining table or special occasions. Fill large, transparent glass jars with an assortment of beautifully decorated cookies. You can even use different jar sizes for a varied height effect. Not only do they add charm to your décor, but they also serve as a convenient way for guests to grab a sweet treat during the event.

Decorating cookies is an artistic activity that allows people to express their creativity and provides sensual enjoyment. The possibilities with food coloring, royal icing, chocolate, and sprinkles are endless. By combining modern home décor skills with creative presentation ideas, people may create a synergistic effect that will wow family and guests. Decorate your surrounds and enjoy your culinary creations.

Chapter 5:
Essential Tools and Equipment

The production of delectable cookies necessitates the use of appropriate materials, processes, as well as instruments and equipment. Regardless of one's level of expertise in baking, the presence of appropriate equipment within the kitchen environment may significantly impact the final results of one's cookie Pres. This section will examine the fundamental tools and equipment required to consistently get optimal results while baking cookies.

Baking Tools and Equipment

1. **Mixing Bowls:** A set of mixing bowls in various sizes is essential for combining ingredients. Stainless steel or glass bowls are great choices as they are easy to clean and won't retain odors.
2. **Measuring Cups and Spoons:** Accurate measurements are crucial in baking. Invest in both dry and liquid measuring cups and a set of measuring spoons for precision.
3. **Whisk:** A whisk is used for mixing dry ingredients, beating eggs, and incorporating air into your cookie dough. A wire whisk with a comfortable handle is a versatile tool in your kitchen.
4. **Spatula:** A rubber spatula is handy for scraping every last bit of dough from the

Chapter 6:
Handy Conversion Tables and Measurement Charts

In the realm of culinary arts, precision plays a key role in both the cooking and baking processes. Regardless of one's level of expertise in the culinary arts, precise measures play a crucial role in ensuring the success of one's culinary endeavors. In the realm of baking, precision encompasses more than just using the suitable components; it requires a comprehensive understanding of various measurements and conversions. This section will provide users with useful conversion tables and measurement charts that may serve as reliable resources throughout the process of cooking. These tools facilitate the conversion of different units of measurement, so ensuring consistent outcomes for your cookies and other baked goods.

Conversion Tables for Precision

One of the first challenges encountered when delving into the realm of baking is the need to do conversions between diverse units of measurement. The presence of several measuring systems, such as the Imperial system, the metric system, or a mix thereof, may be encountered depending on one's geographical location or the provenance of a certain recipe. In order to facilitate seamless navigation through these conversions, we have curated a collection of conversion tables including the frequently used measures in the realm of baking.

Temperature Measurements

One of the first conversions that individuals will come across in the realm of baking pertains to temperature. Certain recipes may provide oven temperatures in Fahrenheit (°F), however others may use Celsius (°C). Proficiency in the conversion between these two systems is crucial for attaining the intended outcomes in the realm of baking.

Fahrenheit to Celsius (°F to °C) Conversion:

- -40°F = -40°C
- -4°F = -20°C
- 32°F = 0°C (Freezing Point)
- 212°F = 100°C (Boiling Point)
- 350°F = 176.67°C (Common Baking Temperature)
- 450°F = 232.22°C (Hot Oven)

Celsius to Fahrenheit (°C to °F) Conversion:

- -40°C = -40°F
- -20°C = -4°F
- 0°C = 32°F (Freezing Point)
- 100°C = 212°F (Boiling Point)
- 150°C = 302°F
- 200°C = 392°F
- 220°C = 428°F

Liquid Measurements

When engaging in the practice of baking, particularly when working with liquid ingredients like as milk, water, or oil, it may be necessary to do conversions between various units of liquid measurement. The conversions most often seen pertain to milliliters (ml), fluid ounces (fl oz), and cups. Presented below is a practical reference table for converting liquid measurements.

Milliliters to Fluid Ounces (ml to fl oz) Conversion:

- 30 ml = 1 fl oz
- 60 ml = 2 fl oz
- 120 ml = 4 fl oz

- 240 ml = 8 fl oz (1 cup)
- 480 ml = 16 fl oz (2 cups)
- 960 ml = 32 fl oz (4 cups or 1 quart)

Fluid Ounces to Milliliters (fl oz to ml) Conversion:

- 1 fl oz = 30 ml
- 2 fl oz = 60 ml
- 4 fl oz = 120 ml
- 8 fl oz = 240 ml (1 cup)
- 16 fl oz = 480 ml (2 cups)
- 32 fl oz = 960 ml (4 cups or 1 quart)

Cups to Milliliters (cups to ml) Conversion:

- 1 cup = 240 ml
- 1/2 cup = 120 ml
- 1/3 cup = 80 ml
- 1/4 cup = 60 ml
- 1/8 cup = 30 ml
- 1/16 cup = 15 ml

Milliliters to Cups (ml to cups) Conversion:

- 240 ml = 1 cup
- 120 ml = 1/2 cup
- 80 ml = 1/3 cup
- 60 ml = 1/4 cup
- 30 ml = 1/8 cup
- 15 ml = 1/16 cup

Baking Measurement Conversions

Apart from temperature and liquid measurements, you'll frequently encounter conversions involving dry ingredients such as flour, sugar, and spices. Here's a comprehensive table to help you convert between various units of measurement commonly used in baking:

Ounces to Grams (oz to g) Conversion:

- 1 oz = 28.35 g

- 2 oz = 56.70 g
- 3 oz = 85.05 g
- 4 oz = 113.40 g
- 5 oz = 141.75 g
- 6 oz = 170.10 g
- 7 oz = 198.45 g
- 8 oz = 226.80 g
- 9 oz = 255.15 g
- 10 oz = 283.50 g

Grams to Ounces (g to oz) Conversion:

- 28.35 g = 1 oz
- 56.70 g = 2 oz
- 85.05 g = 3 oz
- 113.40 g = 4 oz
- 141.75 g = 5 oz
- 170.10 g = 6 oz
- 198.45 g = 7 oz
- 226.80 g = 8 oz
- 255.15 g = 9 oz
- 283.50 g = 10 oz

Cups to Grams (cups to g) Conversion:

- All-purpose flour: 1 cup = 120 g
- Granulated sugar: 1 cup = 200 g
- Brown sugar: 1 cup = 220 g
- Butter: 1 cup = 227 g
- Rolled oats: 1 cup = 90 g
- Powdered sugar: 1 cup = 120 g
- Baking powder: 1 teaspoon = 4 g

These conversion tables are your trusty companions in the kitchen, ensuring that your baking endeavors are precise and successful. Whether you're following a recipe with different units of measurement or adapting a recipe to your specific needs, these tables will help you achieve the accuracy required for outstanding results.

It is important to note that precise measurements have significant importance in the context of baking, as even a little deviation may have a noticeable effect on the texture and flavor of the cookies. When engaging in future baking endeavors, it is advisable to use the provided conversion tables in order to guarantee the desired outcome of your cookies.

In the realm of baking, achieving accuracy is crucial for attaining success. The attainment of optimal texture and flavor in cookies and other baked products is contingent upon the acquisition of precise measurements. The inclusion of conversion tables and measurement charts in your kitchen might prove to be advantageous, as they facilitate the seamless conversion of various units of measurement pertaining to temperature, liquid, and dry materials.

Whether one is a newbie baker aiming to enhance their talents or an expert chef endeavoring to modify recipes according to their own requirements, these conversion tables will guarantee that one's culinary masterpieces are executed with precision. Therefore, when you find yourself in the kitchen again, make use of these tables.

Chapter 7:
40 Delicious Cookie Recipes

Filled Cookies

Cookies with delightful fillings like jam, chocolate, or cream.

Filled Cookies are a delectable treat, known for their irresistible centers bursting with flavor. These delightful confections feature a tender, buttery exterior that cradles an array of sweet surprises, from rich chocolate and velvety cream to luscious fruit jams. Every bite is a symphony of textures and tastes, with the delicate cookie providing a satisfying contrast to the indulgent filling.

Whether you savor the classic combination of chocolate and vanilla, the fruity allure of raspberry jam, or the comforting embrace of a cream-filled delight, these cookies offer a delightful experience for the senses. Filled Cookies are perfect for any occasion, from casual snacking to elegant dessert tables. Enjoy them with a cup of tea, share them with loved ones, or simply relish the joy of biting into a cookie that conceals a hidden treasure of sweetness.

Recipe 1. Caramel-Filled Chocolate Cookies

Servings: 24 | Pre: 20 mins | Cooking: 12 mins

Ingredients:

- 1/2 ounce (14g) caster sugar
- 2 large eggs
- 18 ounces (510g) flour
- 1 teaspoon (5g) bicarbonate of soda
- 4 dozen chocolate-covered caramels (approx. 48 caramels)
- 8 ounces (225g) caster sugar
- 8 ounces (225g) walnuts, chopped
- 1/3 ounce (10ml) vanilla extract
- 8 ounces (225g) packed brown sugar
- 6 ounces (170g) unsweetened cocoa powder
- 8 ounces (225g) softened butte

Directions:

1. Mix butter, brown sugar, and white sugar. Add in the vanilla and eggs to the sugar mixture.

2. Mix cocoa, baking soda, and flour.
3. Toss in 4 ounces of walnuts into your batter.
4. Now, preheat your oven to 375 degrees Fahrenheit. Grab the remaining nuts and ½ ounce of sugar and mix them up in another bowl.
5. Get that dough ball and dunk the top part into the nuts and sugar mixture. Now, place it on a baking sheet with the sugar-covered side facing up. Bake these sweet creations for about 8 mins. After that, take them out and let them cool down. Continue this baking process with the remaining dough in the same delightful way until you've got a batch of delicious cookies to enjoy.

Recipe 2. Raspberry Cream Sugar Cookies

Servings: 18 | Pre: 20 mins | Cooking: 10 mins

Ingredients:

- 1/2 cup (90g) white baking chips
- 6 ounces (170g) cream cheese
- 1/4 cup (60ml) double cream

- 1/4 cup (60g) red raspberry preserves
- 1 large egg
- 1 package sugar cookie mix
- 1/2 cup (115g) butter

Directions:

1. Melt your baking chips with some cream until it's smooth and lump-free.,Pour in your melted baking chip mixture and whisk it until it's smooth. Pop this mixture in the fridge until it firms up.
2. While your filling chills, let's work on the cookies. Mix an egg, some butter, and your cookie mix until everything is well combined.
3. Now that you have your cookies and the filling is chilled, it's time to put them together. Then, put the other halves on top, like little cookie sandwiches.

Recipe 3. Raspberry Vanilla Cookies

Servings: 20 | Pre: 15 mins | Cooking: 10 mins

Ingredients:

- 1/2 cup (115g) butter
- 2 teaspoons (10ml) vanilla extract
- 1 egg

- 1/2 cup (120ml) raspberry jam
- 1 1/2 cups (180g) spelt flour
- 1/3 cup (70g) sugar

Directions:

1. Mix the sugar, butter, egg, and vanilla extract together until creamed. Gently sift the flour into the dough, and when well-mixed, roll the dough into small balls.
2. Bake the cookies for about 10 mins. Let cool before eating.

Recipe 4. Strawberry Ball Cookies

Servings: 30 | Pre: 20 mins | Cooking: 30 mins

Ingredients:

- 1/2 cup (about 75g) strawberries, diced
- 4 tablespoons (about 50g) sugar
- 1/2 cup (about 150g) strawberry jam
- 2 1/4 cups (270g) plain flour

- 1 medium egg
- 4 tablespoons (about 55g) unsalted butter
- 5 tablespoons (about 75ml) milk of your choice
- 1/2 teaspoon (about 2.5g) baking powder
- Zest of 1 lemon

Directions:

1. Mash the strawberries with a fork and mix in the strawberry jam. Set this aside.
2. Mix the sugar, egg, butter, flour, milk, lemon zest, egg, and baking powder until it turns into dough.
3. Place 15 balls on each baking sheet, leaving some space between them. Put one tray in the fridge and bake the other for 20 mins. Let them cool for about 10 mins before digging in. Then, bake the second batch of ball. Enjoy!

Shortbread Cookies

Buttery and crumbly cookies often flavored with vanilla or citrus.

Shortbread cookies, cherished for their irresistible melt-in-your-mouth texture, offer a delightful balance of simplicity and indulgence. These classic treats are characterized by their buttery richness and delicate crumbliness, making every bite a harmonious blend of flavor and texture. Traditionally, shortbread cookies are crafted with just a handful of ingredients, including premium butter, flour, and sugar, allowing the quality of each component to shine.

Shortbread's taste diversity sets it distinct. These cookies' buttery foundation is contrasted with vanilla or citrus flavors in several versions. The cookie's sweetness blends wonderfully with vanilla's flowery overtones or citrus's bright, invigorating taste. Shortbread cookies are a classic delicacy that never fails to provide sheer delight, whether served with tea or alone.

Recipe 5. Almond Shortbread Cookies

Servings: 16 | Pre: 10 mins | Cooking: 25 mins

Ingredients:

- 3 1/2 cups (420g) cake flour
- 1 cup (120g) finely ground almonds
- 1/2 cup (120ml) coconut oil
- 1 cup (120g) icing sugar
- 1 tablespoon (15ml) brandy
- 1/2 cup (120g) almond butter
- 2 egg yolks
- 1 tablespoon (15ml) water or rose flower water
- 1 teaspoon (5ml) vanilla extract

Directions:

1. Start by combining coconut oil, powdered sugar, and butter in a big mixing bowl. If the butter's a bit firm, give it a moment to soften up. Then, blend everything

together using a powerful electric mixer.

2. Mix brandy, water, egg yolks, and vanilla extract. Give it a good whisk.
3. Add in the flour and almonds, and stir it all together with a trusty wooden spoon. Pop that mixture into the fridge for at least 1 hour and 30 mins.
4. Preheat your oven to 325 degrees Fahrenheit.
5. Take your chilled mixture, which should look like dough by now, and shape it into 1-inch balls. Flatten them down a bit with a fork or your fingers.
6. Bake those cookies for about 13 mins, but keep an eye on them to avoid burning. After baking, let the cookies cool for a few mins on a wire rack before enjoying.

Recipe 6. Butter Walnut and Raisin Cookies

Servings: 8 | Pre: 10 mins | Cooking: 15 mins

Ingredients:

- ½ teaspoon (2.5ml) pure almond extract
- 2 tablespoons Truvia
- 1/3 cup (40g) walnuts, ground
- ½ teaspoon (2.5ml) pure vanilla extract

- 2 tablespoons (30ml) rum
- ½ cup (60g) almond flour
- 1 stick (113g) butter
- 1/3 cup (40g) cornflour
- ¼ cup (40g) raisins
- 1 stick (113g) butter

Directions:

1. Beat the butter with Truvia, vanilla, and almond extract until light and fluffy in a mixing dish. Then, throw in both types of flour and ground almonds. Fold in the soaked raisins.
2. Continue mixing until it forms a dough. Refrigerate for approximately 20 mins after covering. Meanwhile, preheat the air-fryer to 330°Fahrenheit. Roll the dough into small cookies, place them in an air-fryer cake pan; gently press each cookie with a spoon. Bake cookies for 15-mins.

Recipe 7. Classic Shortbread Cookies

Servings: 4 | Pre: 20 mins | Cooking: 20 mins

Ingredients:

- 1/3 cup erythritol
- 2 cups (200g) almond flour
- 1/2 cup (113g) unsalted butter

- 1 teaspoon vanilla extract
- 1 pinch salt
- 1 large egg

Directions:

1. As you prepare a cookie sheet, preheat the oven to 300°F.
2. Mix almond flour, vanilla, salt, and erythritol in a mixing dish. Blend well.
3. Beat the egg and add the butter to a different bowl. Combine well.
4. Mix the two parts together until a lump-free, smooth dough is achieved.
5. Bake the cookies for 13 mins. Remove from the oven the cookies. Before consuming, let them cool for about seven mins!

Recipe 8. Lavender Shortbread Cookies

Servings: 24 | Pre: 40 mins | Cooking: 20 mins

Ingredients:

- 4 ounces (115g) cornstarch
- 1 teaspoon lemon zest, grated
- 5 ½ ounces (155g) white sugar
- 20 ounces (570g) flour

- 2 ounces (55g) icing sugar, sifted
- ½ ounce (15g) fresh mint leaves,
- 1/4 teaspoon salt
- 1 ounce (30g) fresh lavender, finely chopped
- 12 ounces (340g) softened butter

Directions:

1. Beat together white sugar, confectioners' sugar, and butter until creamy using an electric mixer.
2. Add lavender, lemon zest, and mint to the sugar mixture.
3. Combine cornstarch, flour, and salt in the same bowl and mix well.
4. Divide the dough into two portions and wrap each in plastic wrap, flattening them to about 1" thickness. Refrigerate for 1 hour.
5. Bake for around 20 mins
6. Allow the cookies to cool on a wire rack before serving. Enjoy!

Chocolate Cookies

Cookies packed with rich and decadent chocolate flavors.

Indulge in the ultimate chocolate lover's delight with our delectable Chocolate Cookies. These treats are a symphony of rich, decadent cocoa flavors that will transport your taste buds to a world of pure chocolatey bliss. Each bite is an exquisite combination of intense dark chocolate and velvety smooth milk chocolate, creating a harmonious balance that's utterly irresistible.

We take great care in crafting our Chocolate Cookies to please even the pickiest palates. They're the ideal textural balance, with a crunchy outside and a soft, oozy within. These are the ultimate chocolate getaway, perfect with a glass of cold milk, as a sweet complement to your afternoon coffee, or as a decadent dessert. Savor the absolute joy of chocolate with every mouthful, and make our Chocolate Cookies your go-to treat for pure, unadulterated chocolate bliss.

Recipe 9. Chocolate-Almond Thumbprint Cookies

Servings: 25 | Pre: 15 mins | Cooking: 20 mins

Ingredients:

- 1 teaspoon baking soda
- 1 medium, ripe banana
- ¼ teaspoon salt
- 1 ½ cups (180g) almond meal or almond flour
- 1 ½ cups (180g) plain unbleached flour
- 2 tablespoons (30g) unsalted butter, plus more for greasing
- 2 tablespoons (30ml) unsweetened applesauce
- ½ cup (100g) caster sugar
- 1 tablespoon (15ml) vanilla extract
- 5 tablespoons chocolate hazelnut spread.

Directions:

1. Preheat your oven to 400°F and line two baking sheets with parchment paper.
2. Peel a banana and mash it up in a small dish using a fork until it's a paste.
3. Mix baking soda, sugar, flour, almond meal, and a pinch of salt with a fork.
4. Slowly add coconut oil, applesauce, your mashed banana, and some vanilla.
5. Grease your hands a bit with coconut oil. Take a spoonful of dough (about 1 tablespoon), roll it into a small ball, and place it on the parchment paper.
6. Bake them in the oven for 20 mins.

Recipe 10. Chocolate Sugar Cookies

Servings: 18 | Pre: 20 mins | Cooking: 12 mins

Ingredients:

- 1 teaspoon (5g) bicarbonate of soda
- 2 (28g) squares unsweetened chocolate, melted
- 1 teaspoon (5g) bicarbonate of soda
- 1/4 cup (60ml) golden syrup (light corn syrup)
- 1 cup (200g) caster sugar
- 2 cups (240g) plain flour
- 1/4 teaspoon (1.25g) salt
- 1 teaspoon (2.5g) ground cinnamon
- 3/4 cup (170g) vegetable shortening
- 1 egg

Directions:

1. Mix sugar, egg, and shortening add melted chocolate and syrup in. Sift ground cinnamon, salt ,baking soda, and flour; add to creamed mixture then chill for an hour.
2. Bake for approximately about 10-12 mins on ungreased cookie sheet.

Recipe 11. Chocolate Waffle Cookies

Servings: 24 | Pre: 10 mins | Cooking: 12 mins

Ingredients:

- 2 (28g) squares semisweet chocolate
- 1 cup (120g) plain flour
- 1/3 cup (75g) butter
- 1 teaspoon (5ml) vanilla extract
- 2 tablespoons (30g) icing sugar
- 2 eggs
- 3/4 cup (150g) caster sugar

Directions:

1. Low heat chocolate and butter mixture, Preheat and grease waffle iron.
2. Beat sugar, vanilla, sugar, vanilla, and eggs. Stir in the chocolate mixture, then stir in the flour mixture gradually until smooth.
3. On the preheated waffle iron, drop batter by heaping spoonful's .
4. Serve after cooling

Recipe 12. Nutella Choc Chip Cookies

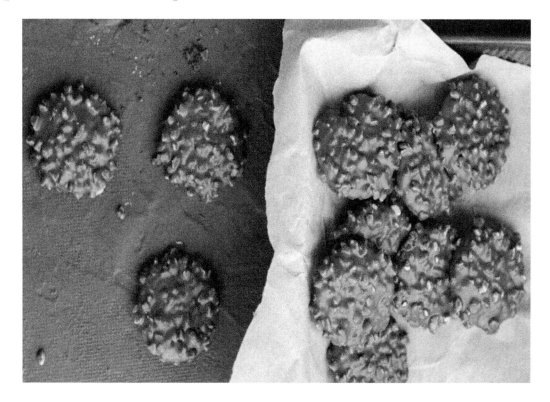

Servings: 32 | Pre: 30 mins | Cooking: 15 mins

Ingredients:

- 1 ¾ cups (210g) of plain flour
- ½ cup (150g) of Nutella spread
- ¾ cup (135g) of chocolate chips
- ½ cup (100g) of light brown sugar
- 1 free-range egg
- 1 cup (225g) of butter
- 1 teaspoon (5g) of baking powder

Directions:

1. Take out beaters and a bowl. Mix sugar and butter.
2. Add Nutella and egg. Beat until mixed through.
3. Sift in flour and baking powder.
4. Add chocolate. Stir with a spoon.
5. Bake for 15 mins.

Frosted Cookies

Cookies adorned with sweet and colorful frosting.

A wonderful delicacy, frosted cookies provide a harmonic fusion of soft, buttery sweetness with bright, sweet icing. These delicious concoctions are a hit with people of all ages since they are visually appealing as well as delicious. The creamy, sweet icing that delicately lays on top of the fragile cookie foundation creates a symphony of tastes and sensations with every mouthful.

The variety of frosted cookies is what gives them their enchantment. They are a treasured addition to birthdays, holidays, and special events as they may be embellished with a kaleidoscope of colors and ornamental designs. Every bite of a frosted cookie, whether it's a rich chocolate cookie topped with glossy ganache or a traditional sugar cookie dappled with pastel colours, is a canvas for creativity. Frosted cookies are a lovely representation of culinary skill and sweetness in every sense, whether they are eaten as a dessert centerpiece, with a cup of hot cocoa, or as an afternoon treat.

Recipe 13. Glazed Pumpkin Drop Cookies

Servings: 30 | Pre: 25 mins | Cooking: 20 mins

Ingredients:

- 1/2 cup (115g) butter
- 1 tablespoon (15g) cinnamon
- 1/2 cup (100g) sugar
- 1 cup (120g) spelt flour
- 1/2 cup (60g) almond flour
- 1/4 teaspoon (1.25g) salt
- 1 1/4 cups (300g) pumpkin purée
- 1/2 teaspoon each (2.5g) ground nutmeg, cloves, and ginger
- 1 teaspoon each (5g) baking powder/baking soda
- 1/2 cup (120ml) applesauce
- 1 egg
- 2 teaspoons (10ml) vanilla extract,
- 1/2 cup (60g) whole wheat flour
- 1 cup (120g) icing sugar

Directions:

1. To begin the baking process, it is recommended to preheat the oven to a temperature of 350°F.
2. In a single bowl, amalgamate the flours, baking powder, baking soda, cinnamon, nutmeg, cloves, ginger, and a little amount of salt.
3. Mix the sugar, applesauce, butter, pumpkin, egg, and 1 teaspoon of vanilla extract until a creamy consistency is achieved.
4. Subsequently, include the dry ingredients into the wet components and thoroughly blend the mixture until a homogeneous consistency is achieved.
5. During the period in which the cookies are through the chilling process, it is recommended to prepare a frosting by combining icing sugar, melted butter, and an additional teaspoon of vanilla extract until a creamy consistency is achieved.
6. After allowing the cookies to cool, proceed to apply the delectable frosting, therefore preparing them for consumption.

Recipe 14. Harvest Sugar Cookies

Servings: 30 | Pre: 15 mins | Cooking: 10 mins

Ingredients:

- 2 eggs
- 1 cup (200g) sugar
- 2-3/4 cups (345g) plain flour
- 1 teaspoon (5g) baking powder

- 3/4 cup (170g) butter
- 1 teaspoon (5ml) vanilla extract
- 1/2 teaspoon (2.5g) salt
- Frosting of your choice or additional sugar (no conversion needed for this ingredient)

Directions:

1. Mix vanilla, and sugar, eggs and butter. Mix baking powder salt, and flour; put to creamed mixture slowly. Let it chill until firm or for 1 hour.
2. Place cookies on a greased baking sheet using a floured spatula. Sprinkle sugar to taste (or frost cooled cookies). Bake for 8–10 mins at 375 degrees until light golden.

Recipe 15. Quilted Sugar Cookies

Servings: 36 | Pre: 20 mins | Cooking: 18 mins

Ingredients:

- 1/2 cup (120g) vanilla frosting and food coloring or decorator's icing
- 1/3 cup (40g) icing sugar (confectioners' sugar)
- 1 large egg
- 3/4 cup (170g) butter

- 1 1/2 cups (180g) plain flour (all-purpose flour)
- 2 tablespoons (30g) sugar

Directions:

1. Mix butter and sugar. Put in eggs; mix thoroughly.
2. Put in flour; stir thoroughly. Let it chill with cover for at least one hour.
3. Use heavy duty foil to line a 15x10x1-inch baking pan. Force dough onto pan's bottom. Use a sharp knife to score dough making squares of 2x2-inches (reroll scraps and bake as directed or get rid of it).
4. Bake for 20 mins the cookies will not turn brown. Use foil to take the cookies off the pan carefully.
5. Slice into squares and let it cool. Use decorator's icing or stir food coloring into frosting to create preferred colors.
6. Use quilt patterns to decorate cookies.

Recipe 16. Soft Frosted Sugar Cookies

Servings: 36 | Pre: 40 mins | Cooking: 15 mins

Ingredients:

- 1 teaspoon (5g) bicarbonate of soda
- 1/4 cup (55g) butter
- 1 1/2 teaspoons (7.5ml) vanilla extract
- 1/4 cup (60ml) milk

- 2 eggs
- 1 cup (200g) caster sugar
- 3 cups (360g) plain flour
- 1 teaspoon (5g) salt
- 3 cups (360g) icing sugar
- 1 cup (225g) vegetable shortening
- 2 tablespoons (30ml) milk

Directions:

1. Mix the 1/4 cup (60ml) of milk and bicarbonate of soda.
2. Mix the 1 cup (225g) of vegetable shortening, butter, eggs, and caster sugar
3. Stir in the vanilla extract.
4. Mix the salt and plain flour. Add the dry ingredients to the wet ingredients.
5. Now, pour in the milk and bicarbonate of soda mixture that you set aside earlier. Mix until well combined.
6. Scoop out tablespoon-sized portions of dough and roll them into balls. Place the dough balls onto the prepared baking sheet, leaving some space between each one.
7. Use the bottom of a glass or a flat surface to gently flatten each dough ball into a round cookie shape.
8. Bake in the preheated oven for approximately 10-12 minutes, or until the edges of the cookies start to turn golden brown.
9. While the cookies are baking, prepare the frosting. In a mixing bowl, combine the remaining 1 cup (225g) of vegetable shortening, icing sugar, and 2 tablespoons (30ml) of milk. Beat until the frosting is smooth and creamy.
10. Bake for 15 minutes.

Fluffy Cookies

Light and airy cookies with a melt-in-your-mouth texture.

With each mouthful, fluffy cookies provide a wonderful experience that will tantalize your taste senses. The magic that can be worked in the realm of baking is shown by these cookies. They gently crumble and melt in your tongue thanks to their light and airy nature, leaving a path of pure ecstasy in their wake.

Imagine sinking your teeth into a cloud of sweetness, as these cookies delicately disintegrate, releasing their subtle, buttery aroma. Each bite is a symphony of flavors and textures, as the fluffy cookies blend the perfect balance of sweetness and tenderness.

Whether enjoyed with a cup of hot tea, a glass of milk, or simply on their own, these cookies are a heartwarming treat that promises to elevate your snacking experience. Savor the ethereal sensation of Fluffy Cookies and let them transport you to a world of pure cookie perfection.

Recipe 17. Coconut Cookies

Servings: 15 | Pre: 10 mins | Cooking: 10 mins

Ingredients:

- 3/4 cup (90g) coconut flour
- 2 cups (480g) smooth cashew butter
- 1/2 cup (120ml) pure maple syrup
- 1-2 tablespoons (15-30g) sprinkles

Directions:

1. Put the coconut flour in a bowl.
2. Mix in the cashew butter and maple syrup until it's all nicely blended.
3. Throw in those sprinkles and give it a good stir.
4. If the batter's too thin, toss in a bit more coconut flour.

5. On the flip side, if it's too thick, add a touch of water.
6. Shape that batter into small balls and place them on your parchment paper.
7. Flatten those balls into cookie shapes.
8. Let 'em chill for a bit, then serve 'em up! Enjoy!

Recipe 18. Melt-In-Your-Mouth Sugar Cookies

Servings: 48 | Pre: 3 hours 20 mins | Cooking: 15 mins

Ingredients:

- 3 ounces (85g) cream cheese
- 1/2 teaspoon (2.5ml) vanilla extract
- 1 cup (200g) sugar
- 1 large egg yolk
- 1/4 teaspoon (1.25ml) almond extract
- 1 cup (225g) butter
- 2-1/4 cups (270g) plain flour
- 1/2 teaspoon (2.5g) salt
- 1/4 teaspoon (1.25g) baking soda
- Tinted frosting, coarse sugar, and/or coloured sugar (no conversion needed for these)

Directions:

1. Whisk together sugar, cream cheese, and butter in a large mixing bowl until fluffy and light. Mix in extracts and egg yolk. Stir baking soda, salt, and flour together; slowly mix into creamed mixture.
2. Arrange cookies on ungreased baking sheets, separating them 1 inch apart. Bake cookies for 8 to 10 mins at 375°, until edges start browning. Garnish cookies if desired.

Recipe 19. Peanut Butter Cookies

Servings: 2 | Pre: 10 mins | Cooking: 13 mins

Ingredients:

- 1 teaspoon (5ml) vanilla extract
- 1 teaspoon (5g) bicarbonate of soda
- 1 cup (120g) whole wheat flour
- 1/4 teaspoon (1.25g) salt
- 1/2 cup (170g) honey
- 1/3 cup (80ml) plain unsweetened non-dairy milk
- 1 cup (240g) creamy peanut butter

Directions:

1. In a large basin, mix the flour, baking soda, and salt. In a second dish, mix the peanut butter, honey, nondairy milk, and vanilla.
2. Combine the wet and dry components with clean or gloved hands. The dough will be too stiff to mix with a spoon. Knead the dough until there are no patches of dry ingredients remaining.
3. Make 24 balls, each with 1 heaping tablespoon of dough.
4. Bake the cookies for 10 mins for a chewy texture or 12 to 13 mins for crispier cookies.

Recipe 20. Pumpkin Oatmeal Raisin Cookies

Servings: 20 | Pre: 10 mins | Cooking: 11 mins

Ingredients:

- ¾ cup (120g) raisins
- 2 teaspoons (10g) ground cinnamon
- 1 teaspoon (5g) baking soda
- 1 cup (90g) old-fashioned rolled oats
- 1 teaspoon (5g) pumpkin pie spice
- ¾ cup (150g) packed dark brown sugar
- 2 teaspoons (10ml) pure vanilla extract
- 2 cups (240g) whole wheat flour
- ½ teaspoon (2.5g) kosher salt or sea salt

- 1 cup (90g) old-fashioned rolled oats
- 1 teaspoon (5g) baking powder
- ¼ cup (55g) unsalted butter, softened
- 2 large eggs
- 1½ cups (360ml) pumpkin purée

Directions:

1. Start by getting your ingredients ready. You'll need cinnamon, flour, baking soda, salt, oats, pumpkin pie spice, baking powder, brown sugar, butter, eggs, pumpkin purée, vanilla extract, and some raisins.
2. In a medium-sized mixing bowl, combine the cinnamon, flour, baking soda, salt, oats, pumpkin pie spice, and baking powder. Mix them all together.
3. Mix butter and the brown sugar. Mix the pumpkin purée, eggs, and vanilla extract. Slowly add the dry ingredients from the first bowl into the large one with the wet ingredients. Mix them together just until they're combined. Don't forget to gently fold in raisins.
4. Time to preheat your oven to 350°F. While it's heating up, grab a baking sheet and line it with parchment paper.
5. Pop them into the preheated oven and bake for about 8 to 11 mins. You want them to start turning slightly brown around the edges.

Dry and Crispy Cookies

Crunchy cookies that are perfect for dunking in milk or tea.

Indulge in the delightful world of Dry and Crispy Cookies, where every bite delivers a satisfying crunch and a burst of flavor. These cookies are the epitome of textural perfection, with a delicate crispiness that makes them ideal companions for your daily tea or milk ritual. Whether you're a fan of a subtle, buttery crunch or a heartier, nutty bite, this category of cookies offers an array of options to suit your taste.

Picture yourself savoring a golden, caramelized almond biscotti with a steaming cup of espresso or dipping a classic shortbread cookie into a glass of ice-cold milk. These cookies are not just a treat for your taste buds; they're also a delightful sensory experience. Their dry, crunchy nature invites you to take your time, enjoying each bite as it melts in your mouth. So, go ahead and explore the world of Dry and Crispy Cookies – they're the perfect balance of simplicity and satisfaction, designed to elevate your everyday moments of indulgence.

Recipe 21. Crisp Little Lemon Cookies

Servings: 48 | Pre: 25 mins | Cooking: 12 mins

Ingredients:

- 240ml crisp rice cereal
- 1 (518g) package lemon cake mix
- 1 egg
- 115g butter

Directions:

1. Combine crunchy rice cereal and cake mix in a medium-sized bowl. Incorporate the liquefied butter and egg into the mixture until a thorough amalgamation is achieved.
2. Form the mixture into spherical shapes with a diameter of 1 inch, ensuring that they are evenly spaced around 2 inches apart on a baking sheet that has not been coated with any kind of oil. Place the mixture in the oven that has been warmed and let it to bake for a duration of 10 to 12 mins.
3. Following the baking process, it is recommended to allow the cookies to cool on the cookie sheets for a little period of time, about one minute, before transferring them onto wire racks to facilitate thorough cooling.

Recipe 22. Ginger Crisp Cookies

Servings: 36 | Pre: 22 mins | Cooking: 17 mins

Ingredients:

- 2 teaspoons (10g) bicarbonate of soda
- 1 pinch nutmeg
- 4 drops stevia extract
- 2 eggs
- 1 1/2 teaspoons (7.5g) ground ginger
- 1/2 cup (115g) butter
- 1/4 cup (60ml) vegetable oil
- 3 cups (360g) plain flour
- 1 pinch salt
- 1/2 teaspoon (2.5g) ground cinnamon

Directions:

1. Mix butter and add the stevia extract. Stir in the oil then add the eggs and give it a good mix.
2. Add in the ginger, baking soda, cinnamon, salt, flour, and nutmeg.
3. Give it a quick mix just until well combined then drop spoonfuls of batter on 2-3 baking sheets lined with parchment paper.
4. Bake for 18 mins.

Recipe 23. Maple Sugar Cookies

Servings: 48 | Pre: 20 mins | Cooking: 12 mins

Ingredients:

- 1/4 cup (60ml) maple syrup
- 3/4 teaspoon (3.75g) baking powder
- 1-1/4 cups (250g) sugar
- 2 eggs
- 3 cups (360g) plain flour
- 3 teaspoons (15ml) vanilla extract
- 1 cup (240g) butter-flavored shortening
- 1/2 teaspoon (2.5g) baking soda
- 1/2 teaspoon (2.5g) salt

Directions:

1. Mix the sugar and the eggs add the syrup and vanilla. Mix the rest of the ingredients; slowly put into creamed mixture and combine thoroughly. Chill with cover till handleable, for about 2 hours.
2. Arrange on unoiled baking sheets, an-inch away.
3. Bake for approximately about 9 to 12 mins at 350° . Transfer onto wire racks and let cool.

Recipe 24. Nutty Crisp Sugar Cookies

Servings: 60 | Pre: 30 mins | Cooking: 15 mins

Ingredients:

- 1/4 teaspoon (1.25g) salt
- 3/4 cup (90g) walnuts
- 1 teaspoon (5ml) vanilla extract
- 1 cup (225g) butter
- 5 cups (600g) plain flour
- 2 teaspoons (10g) cream of tartar
- 2 cups (400g) caster sugar
- 2 teaspoons (10g) bicarbonate of soda
- 2 eggs
- 1 cup (240ml) vegetable oil
- 2 teaspoons (10g) bicarbonate of soda

Directions:

1. Heat an oven to a heat of 175 ° C or 350 ° F. Oil cookie sheets lightly. Mix salt, cream of tartar, baking soda and flour; put aside.
2. Mix butter and sugar. Whip in vegetable oil, vanilla and eggs. Slowly mix in mixture of flour till smooth. Mix nuts in. Drop rounded teaspoonfuls of dough.
3. Bake till the edges start to turn brown.

International Cookies

Explore cookie recipes from around the world, each with its unique twist.

Dive into the captivating world of International Cookies, where the enticing aroma of global flavors fills your kitchen. This chapter takes you on a delectable journey around the world, offering a delightful array of cookie recipes, each with its own distinctive twist. From the rich and buttery shortbread of Scotland to the delicate almond crescents of Germany, these recipes transport your taste buds to far-off places without leaving your home.

Discover the secrets behind the perfect Italian biscotti, the exotic allure of Moroccan almond pastries, and the comforting nostalgia of American chocolate chip cookies. International Cookies is your passport to a sweet adventure, allowing you to savor the diverse flavors and traditions that cookies embody across cultures. Whether you're a seasoned baker or a novice, these recipes are an invitation to explore, create, and share the universal joy of cookies with a global twist. So, don your apron and embark on a delicious expedition that transcends borders and celebrates the universal love for cookies.

Recipe 25. All American Choc Chip Cookies

Servings: 36 | Pre: 18 mins | Cooking: 10 mins

Ingredients:

- 1 cup (200g) light brown sugar
- 1 cup (240g) salted butter
- 1 teaspoon bicarbonate of soda (baking soda)
- 1 (340g) package chocolate chips
- 2 eggs
- 2 cups (240g) flour
- 1 cup (200g) granulated sugar
- 2 cups (200g) quick-cooking oats
- 2 teaspoons vanilla extract
- 1 cup (240g) salted butter

Directions:

1. Start by preheating your main oven to 350°F.
2. Mix the butter, light brown sugar, and granulated sugar.
3. Add the eggs and give them a good beat until everything's nicely combined.
4. Mix flour and the baking soda. Now, add this flour mix to your egg mix.
5. Time to toss in the oats, followed by the vanilla extract and those delicious chocolate chips.
6. Pop those cookie-filled sheets into the oven and bake for about 10 mins.
7. Once they're out, let them cool a bit before digging in.

Recipe 26. Mexican Chocolate Sugar Cookies

Servings: 48 | Pre: 25 mins | Cooking: 20 mins

Ingredients:

- 1/4 teaspoon (1.25g) salt
- 1-1/2 teaspoons (1.5g) ground cinnamon
- 1 large egg
- 2 ounces (57g) unsweetened chocolate
- 1 cup (170g) semisweet chocolate chips
- 1/4 cup (60ml) light corn syrup
- 1-3/4 cups (220g) plain flour
- 1-1/4 cups (250g) sugar
- 3/4 cup (170g) vegetable shortening
- 1 teaspoon (5g) bicarbonate of soda

Directions:

1. Mix the shortening and 1 cup sugar. Add in corn syrup, melted chocolate, and egg. Combine cinnamon, salt, baking soda and flour together; slowly add to creamed mixture and beat well; fold in chocolate chips.
2. Bake cookies in the preheated oven until top puffs and start cracks, for 8 to 10 mins.
3. Cookie dough can actually be prepared 2 days ahead.
4. Wrap cookies in plastic wrap and put into a resealable bag. Keep chilled in the

fridge.

5. For freeze option: freeze shaped dough balls on baking sheets until hardened. Remove to resealable plastic freezer bags; put back into the freezer. When using, bake cookies according to directions.

Recipe 27. Moravian Sugar Cookies

Servings: 30 | Pre: 25 mins | Cooking: 10 mins

Ingredients:

- 1 teaspoon (2.5g) ground cinnamon
- 1 1/2 cups (360ml) dark molasses
- 1/4 teaspoon (1.25g) bicarbonate of soda
- 1/2 cup (115g) shortening
- 1/4 teaspoon (1.25g) salt
- 1/4 teaspoon (0.6g) ground ginger
- 1 cup (200g) packed brown sugar
- 4 1/2 cups (540g) plain flour
- 1/2 cup (115g) butter
- 1/2 teaspoon (1.25g) ground cloves

- 1/2 teaspoon (2.5ml) distilled white vinegar
- 1 teaspoon (2.5g) ground cinnamon

Directions:

1. First, combine ginger, cloves, cinnamon, salt, baking soda, and flour in a bowl.
2. In another basin, whisk shortening, butter, and brown sugar.
3. Blend this mixture into the dry ingredients until fully combined.
4. Pour in vinegar and molasses and mix. Keep dough covered in the fridge overnight.
5. Bake the cookie forms for 10 mins at 180°C (350°F) until light golden.

Recipe 28. South African Chocolate Pepper Cookies

Servings: 5 | Pre: 15 mins | Cooking: 15 mins

Ingredients:

- 12 tablespoons (170g) of butter
- 1 tablespoon of freshly ground black pepper
- 2 large eggs
- 1 pound (453g) of bittersweet or semi-sweet chocolate
- 2 cups (240g) of plain flour

- 2/3 cup (133g) of brown sugar
- 2/3 teaspoon (about 2g) of bicarbonate of soda

Directions:

1. Melt butter, Add sugar and stir until completely blended after beating the margarine until light and fluffy.
2. Be careful to stir thoroughly after adding each egg.
3. Sift or whisk flour and baking soda in another basin. Mix the dry ingredients into the margarine mixture gently on low speed until just combined.
4. Add melted chocolate to the butter mixture. Add the remaining chopped chocolate and ground pepper.
5. Bake for 10–12 mins until crispy exterior, chewy interior.

Eggless Cookies

Cookie recipes for those looking to skip eggs, with equally delicious results.

Indulge in the delightful world of Eggless Cookies, where the absence of eggs doesn't mean sacrificing taste or texture. In this collection of mouthwatering recipes, we've curated a selection of treats that cater to both egg-free bakers and cookie enthusiasts. Whether you're vegan, have dietary restrictions, or simply ran out of eggs, these recipes are your passport to cookie bliss.

Discover the magic of ingredient substitutions and innovative techniques that bring out the best in each cookie. From classic chocolate chip cookies to exotic flavors like lavender-infused shortbreads, you'll find a wide array of options to satisfy your sweet cravings. Dive into the realm of Eggless Cookies and embark on a delicious journey that proves you can have your cookie and eat it too, sans eggs. These recipes promise the same chewy, crunchy, or melt-in-your-mouth goodness, all without a single egg in sight.

Recipe 29. Coffee Sugar Cookies

Servings: 12 | Pre: 10 mins | Cooking: 12 mins

Ingredients:

- 2 cups (240g) plain flour
- 1 cup (200g) granulated sugar
- 2 tablespoons (20g) ground coffee
- 1 pinch sea salt
- 1 teaspoon (5g) baking powder
- 4 tablespoons (60ml) milk
- 1 teaspoon (5ml) coffee extract
- 1 cup (240ml) vegetable oil

Directions:

1. First, preheat your oven to 400°F. Grab a cookie sheet and line it with parchment paper. Take some vegetable oil and sugar, then give them a good mix.
2. Keep mixing until that sugar completely dissolves.
3. Now, pour in the milk and coffee extract, and mix that up real good.
4. Add in the baking powder, ground coffee, sea salt, and all-purpose flour.

5. Roll up your sleeves and knead that dough for a solid 5 mins. Then, let it chill out in the fridge for a bit. Roll out the dough and cut it into rounds.
6. Pop 'em in the oven for about 12 mins. Once they're done, let 'em cool down, and you're good to go! Enjoy your treats.

Recipe 30. Matcha Blueberry Cookies

Servings: 12 | Pre: 25 mins | Cooking: 12 mins

Ingredients:

- 1 cup (120g) plain flour
- 1/3 cup (40g) matcha powder
- 1 teaspoon (5g) baking powder
- 1 pinch salt
- 1/2 cup (120ml) vegetable oil
- 2 tablespoons (30ml) milk
- 1/2 cup (100g) sugar
- 1 teaspoon (5ml) blueberry extract
- 1/3 cup (40g) fresh blueberries

Directions:

1. First, sift together your all-purpose flour, a pinch of salt, some matcha powder, and baking powder.

2. In another bowl, take your sugar and vegetable oil and give them a good mix.
3. Now, pour in your milk and add a touch of blueberry extract. Give it another good mix. Grab those sifted ingredients and add them in. Carefully fold everything together until it forms a dough.
4. Pop that dough in the fridge and let it chill for a cozy 20 mins.
5. Once it's had its rest, toss in some blueberries and give it another fold.
6. Take spoonfuls of the mixture and plop them onto a prepared cookie sheet.
7. Slide that sheet into the oven and bake for about 12 mins.

Recipe 31. Pumpkin Spice Cookies

Servings: 24 | Pre: 40 mins | Cooking: 30 mins

Ingredients:

- 1 tablespoon (15ml) pumpkin pie spice
- 2 cups (200g) almond meal
- 1/2 teaspoon (2.5g) baking soda
- 1/2 teaspoon (2.5g) fine sea salt
- 1/2 cup (120ml) pumpkin puree
- 1 tablespoon (15ml) vanilla extract
- 1/3 cup (80ml) melted coconut oil
- 3 tablespoons (45ml) Splenda
- 1 banana, mashed

Directions:

1. Initially, combine all the constituent elements, afterwards amalgamate them with liquefied coconut oil.
2. Using a spoon, extract portions of the dough and carefully position them onto a baking sheet that has been covered with parchment paper.
3. Carefully apply pressure to each portion of dough in order to gently decrease its thickness. Next, it is recommended to preheat the oven to a temperature of 350°F.
4. After the oven has reached the desired temperature, carefully place the cookie sheet with the prepared dough inside and begin baking for around 30 mins.
5. Upon completion of the baking process, it is recommended to remove the cookies from the oven and allow them to cool for about 10 mins. Subsequently, the prepared items are in a state of readiness to be presented and savored.

Recipe 32. Vegan Almond Flour Sugar Cookies

Servings: 20 | Pre: 45 mins | Cooking: 20 mins

Ingredients:

- 2 tablespoons (30g) coconut butter
- 1/4 cup (60ml) agave syrup
- 1 teaspoon (5g) baking powder
- 1 teaspoon (5ml) vanilla extract
- 1 pinch salt
- 2 1/2 cups (300g) blanched almond flour

72

Directions:

1. In a food processor, toss in some salt, baking powder, vanilla extract, melted coconut butter, agave syrup, and almond flour. Give it a whirl until you get a nice, soft dough. Wrap that dough up with some plastic wrap and let it chill in the fridge for about 30 mins.
2. Once your dough is chilled, roll it out until it's about a quarter-inch thick. Grab your favorite cookie cutter and make some cookie shapes. Place these on the baking sheet you prepared earlier.
3. Bake for around 12 to 14 mins. Keep an eye on them – you'll know they're ready when they turn a light golden color. Enjoy your homemade cookies!

Original Cookies

Get creative with cookies using unusual ingredients like cheese or green tea.

Unleash your inner cookie maverick with our Original Cookies chapter, where we redefine the boundaries of traditional baking. Discover the delightful surprise of savory and sweet, as ingredients like cheese add unexpected depth to your treats. These savory cheese-infused cookies are an exquisite fusion of creamy and crunchy, perfect for those who crave a unique flavor profile.

For the more adventurous, our green tea-inspired creations will transport your taste buds to the tranquil gardens of Japan. Earthy and slightly bitter, green tea adds an exquisite twist to the classic cookie, offering a taste that's both calming and captivating. Dive into these innovative recipes and let your creativity flourish in the world of unconventional cookie delights. Elevate your baking game and redefine what cookies can be with Original Cookies.

Recipe 33. Honey Sesame Cookies

Servings: 2 | Pre: 10 mins | Cooking: 15 mins

Ingredients:

- 3 cups (360g) flour
- 1 tablespoon (15ml) vinegar
- 1 cup (200g) sugar
- 1 cup (225g) butter
- 2 eggs
- 1 teaspoon (5ml) vanilla extract
- 3 tablespoons (45ml) honey
- 1 cup (120g) pistachio nuts, roughly chopped
- 1 cup (120g) sesame seeds
- 1 teaspoon (5g) baking powder
- A pinch of salt

Directions:

1. Mix sugar and butter till light and fluffy. Next, carefully whisk in the eggs, vanilla, and vinegar. Mix salt, flour, and baking powder in a large basin until just mixed. Put this mixture in the fridge for an hour covered.
2. Let's make those scrumptious cookies. Mix sesame seeds and honey on a medium

dish. On another dish, put pistachios. Form a ball from a teaspoon of cooled dough and roll it in pistachios. Press it and dip it in sesame-honey. Repeat with the remaining dough and place the cookies on a baking sheet.

3. Bake the cookies for 15 mins.

Recipe 34. Pear Cookies

Servings: 36 | Pre: 40 mins | Cooking: 20 mins

Ingredients:

- 3/4 cup (170g) butter
- 1/4 teaspoon (1.25g) ground cinnamon
- 1 teaspoon (5ml) orange zest
- 2 eggs
- 1 teaspoon (5g) baking soda
- 1/2 cup (120g) applesauce
- 1/4 cup (60ml) fresh orange juice
- 1 1/2 cups (180g) plain flour
- 1 cup (90g) rolled oats
- 1/2 teaspoon (2.5g) baking powder
- 3/4 cup (170g) butter
- 1 teaspoon (5ml) vanilla extract
- 2 ripe pears, peeled and diced
- 2 shelled walnuts

Directions:

1. Combine butter and orange zest in a bowl and mix for 5 mins until creamy.
2. Stir in the eggs, followed by the applesauce and orange juice and mix well. Stir in the flour, oats, baking soda, baking powder and cinnamon then fold in the pears.
3. Drop spoonfuls of batter on your prepared baking pans and bake for 15-20 mins or until golden brown on the edges.
4. When done, remove from the preheated oven and cool the cookies on wire racks.

Recipe 35. Walnut Cookies

Servings: 10 | Pre: 10 mins | Cooking: 8 mins

Ingredients:

- 2 ½ cups (300g) of ground walnuts
- 1 tablespoon (15g) of softened butter
- 2 teaspoons (10ml) of orange marmalade
- 1/3 cup (67g) of sugar
- 2 beaten eggs
- 1 teaspoon (5g) of baking powder
- 1/4 cup (30g) of icing sugar (confectioner's sugar)

Directions:

1. Mix sugar and walnuts in a bowl.
2. Next, add sugar, butter, and orange marmalade to the bowl. Stir in the two eggs until you have a dough-like mixture. Allow the mixture to sit for about 5 mins.
3. After that, add the baking powder and more eggs. Shape the dough into small balls and coat them with confectioner's sugar. Place these cookie balls onto a baking sheet.
4. Bake for 8 mins.

Recipe 36. Pumpkin Pecan Pie Cookies

Servings: 8 | Pre: 12 mins | Cooking: 18 mins

Ingredients:

- 1 cup (120g) almond flour
- 1/2 cup (85g) Medjool dates
- 2 tablespoons (30ml) granulated sugar
- 1/4 teaspoon (1.25g) salt
- Pecans - enough for all the cookies (pecans are typically not converted, as they are a type of nut and can be used as-is)

Directions:

1. Throw all the ingredients, except the pecans, into your blender and give them a

good whirl.
2. Once it's all mixed up, scoop out the dough and bring it together into a ball.
3. Now, cut that dough into small balls and press 'em down with a fork.
4. Time to pop those pecans in, then bake until they turn a nice golden brown.
5. Finally, stash your tasty treats in an airtight container to keep 'em fresh. Enjoy!

Sugar-Free Cookies

Cookies sweetened without traditional sugar, perfect for those seeking healthier options.

Experience guilt-free indulgence with our assortment of Sugar-Free Cookies. Designed to cater to those who possess a preference for saccharine flavors and a fervor for maintaining a wholesome lifestyle, these cookies provide a remarkable sensory experience devoid of the customary surge in blood glucose levels associated with conventional sugary treats. A selection of dishes has been carefully chosen, using natural sweeteners with minimal calorie content, in order to satisfy cravings for sweetness while maintaining control over sugar intake.

Each bite is a delightful journey through a symphony of tastes, from rich chocolatey goodness to nutty, spiced, or fruity sensations, all expertly balanced to cater to your cravings without the sugar overload. Whether you're managing diabetes, embracing a low-carb lifestyle, or simply seeking a healthier alternative, our Sugar-Free Cookies offer a scrumptious way to enjoy life's little indulgences. Discover a world where sweetness and health coexist harmoniously, one bite at a time.

Recipe 37. Cashew Butter Cookies

Servings: 20 | Pre: 15 mins | Cooking: 17 mins

Ingredients:

- 1 cup (240g) creamy cashew butter
- 1/4 teaspoon (1.25g) salt
- 1/4 cup (60ml) maple syrup
- 1/4 cup (30g) ground flaxseed

Directions:

1. Add the cashew butter, salt, flaxseed, and maple syrup to a large mixing bowl. Combine till the mixture is creamy and smooth.
2. Prepare the oven by actually preheating it to a heat of 350 degrees F.
3. Bake for about 17 mins till the cookies get set properly. Transfer to a tray and allow to cool down.
4. Serve right away or actually save for later in airtight containers.

Recipe 38. Sesame Raisin Cookies

Servings: 8 | Pre: 15 mins | Cooking: 25 mins

Ingredients:

- 1/2 cup (75g) raisins
- 1 1/8 cups (270ml) unsweetened apple juice
- 1/2 cup (70g) sesame seeds
- 1 cup (120g) brown rice flour
- 1/4 teaspoon (1.25g) salt
- 3/4 cup (180ml) water
- 1 teaspoon (5ml) vanilla extract
- 2 tablespoons (30ml) vegetable oil
- 1 1/4 cups (125g) rolled oats

Directions:

1. Boil 3/4 cup of water, add the raisins, and let them soak for at least ten mins. Afterward, drain and roughly chop the plumped-up raisins.
2. Take a heavy sauté pan and put it on medium heat. Keep at it for about 10 mins.
3. Combine the toasted sesame seeds with salt, oats, and rice flour. Mix in the oil, vanilla, and apple juice until everything is well blended.
4. Shape the dough into eight large balls and place them on greased parchment paper or cookie sheets.
5. Bake for 25 mins. Let the cookies cool on the pans for a bit, and then you can remove and enjoy them.

Recipe 39. Lemon Cardamom Cookies

Servings: 4 | Pre: 15 mins | Cooking: 15 mins

Ingredients:

- 1/2 cup (100g) granulated sweetener
- 1/4 teaspoon (0.25g) clementine or lemon zest
- 6 tablespoons (85g) butter, melted
- 1/4 teaspoon (0.25g) ground cardamom
- 2 cups (240g) almond flour
- 2 ounces (56g) dark chocolate (90% or more)

Directions:

1. Preheat the oven to 350°F. Line a cookie sheet with parchment paper.
2. Add the sweetener, cardamom, butter, almond flour, and zest to a mixing bowl. Mix into a smooth dough. Refrigerate for 10 mins.
3. Place the cookies on the cookie sheet. Bake for 14–15 mins until golden brown.
4. Remove cookies from the preheated oven and let cool for 5–10 mins.
5. Melt the chocolate in the microwave until fully melted (about 1 minute).
6. Dip the actual bottom half of each cookie in the prepared melted chocolate. Set aside for a while until chocolate is firm.

Recipe 40. Sugar-Free Date Cookies

Servings: 18 | Pre: 22 mins | Cooking: 12 mins

Ingredients:

- 1 large egg
- 1/4 cup (30g) pecans
- 1 teaspoon (5g) ground cinnamon
- 1/2 very ripe banana, mashed
- 1 cup (120g) plain flour
- 1 cup (120g) dates
- 2 tablespoons (30g) butter
- 1/2 teaspoon (2.5ml) vanilla extract
- 1 teaspoon (5g) salt
- 1/4 cup (60ml) water
- 1 large egg
- 1 teaspoon (5g) baking powder

Directions:

1. Prepare the oven by actually preheating it to a heat of 350 degrees F. Also, use parchment paper for lining a baking sheet for later use.
2. Mix banana, egg, butter, the pecans, dates, vanilla, and water; combine well.
3. In another bowl, beat the baking powder, cinnamon, flour, and salt. Add the date mixture to this mixture and stir till a combined dough is formed.
4. Transfer the prepared sheet to the oven and bake for about 10-12 mins till the cookies get set and golden brown.
5. Once ready, take them out of the preheated oven and let them cool down for a while. Serve immediately or store in airtight containers.

BONUS:
10 Festive Christmas Cookie Recipes

The Christmas season is characterized by a sense of unity, happiness, and undoubtedly, delectable indulgences. When contemplating the Christmas season, a prominent aspect that readily springs to consciousness is the delightful realm of Christmas cookies. These little baked delicacies possess the ability to elicit smiles, conjure nostalgic recollections, and propagate a sense of celebratory ambiance unlike any other.

In this supplementary chapter, we will explore the captivating domain of Christmas cookies. These confections transcend their mere culinary nature, embodying cultural customs, affection, and a hint of enchantment inside each delectable morsel. Christmas cookies evoke a sense of sentimentality, whether they are intended to be left out for Santa Claus or shared with cherished individuals in the cozy ambiance of a fireplace.

Holiday Favorites

1. **Classic Gingerbread Cookies:** Let us start with a genuine Yuletide staple - gingerbread biscuits. These cookies have been a traditional part of Christmas celebrations for several generations. The olfactory sensation of the pleasant and comforting blend of ginger, cinnamon, and nutmeg permeating one's living space throughout the baking process is capable of evoking a sense of festivity in individuals. The process of adorning gingerbread people with vibrant frosting and

confectionery embellishments is a beloved tradition practiced by families around the globe.

2. **Peppermint Meltaways:** What is the celebration of Christmas without a subtle infusion of peppermint flavor? The cookies possess a delightful texture that effortlessly dissolves upon contact with the palate, achieving an optimal equilibrium between saccharine and invigorating flavors. Typically, these confections are coated with a fine layer of powdered sugar and embellished with a decorative candy cane kiss in either red or green.

3. **Snowball Cookies (Mexican Wedding Cookies):** These tender, buttery cookies are rolled in powdered sugar, resembling tiny snowballs. They crumble beautifully in your mouth, leaving a sweet, nutty flavor behind.

4. **Linzer Cookies:** If you're looking for a more sophisticated cookie for your holiday platter, Linzer cookies are an excellent choice. These are sandwich cookies with a sweet jam filling peeking through the center cutout. Their delicate, nutty flavor and vibrant appearance make them a hit at holiday gatherings.

5. **Chocolate Crinkle Cookies:** For those who have a fondness for chocolate, few things can compare to the delectable experience of indulging in a serving of chocolate crinkle cookies. The cookies possess an aesthetically pleasing crackling look as a result of being coated in powdered sugar before to the baking process. These brownies possess a significant level of affluence, a dense texture, and an exceedingly indulgent quality.

Festive Cookie Delights

1. **Cranberry White Chocolate Cookies:** These cookies combine the tartness of dried cranberries with the sweetness of white chocolate chips. The result? A delightful dance of flavors and textures that scream Christmas.

2. **Eggnog Cookies:** Regardless of personal preferences, eggnog is widely regarded as a traditional and essential beverage during the Christmas season. If one aligns with the perspective of favoring eggnog, they will really like eggnog cookies. The bite-sized dessert successfully encapsulates the rich and flavorful characteristics of this traditional beverage associated with celebrations.

3. **Red Velvet Crinkle Cookies:** Red velvet is synonymous with celebrations, and Christmas is no exception. These crimson cookies have a soft, cake-like texture and are rolled in powdered sugar for that irresistible crinkle effect. A drizzle of cream cheese icing on top adds the perfect finishing touch.

4. **Chocolate-Dipped Shortbread:** Shortbread cookies are a simple pleasure, and when dipped in rich, melted chocolate, they become a holiday delight. You can get creative with toppings like crushed candy canes, chopped nuts, or even a sprinkle of edible gold dust for a touch of elegance.

5. **Holiday Spritz Cookies:** Spritz cookies are a fun and colorful addition to any

holiday cookie platter. These buttery delights are piped through a cookie press into various festive shapes, making them a favorite among kids and adults alike.

10 Christmas Season Cookie Favorites

Recipe 1. Cherry Fruitcake Cookies

Servings: 20 | Pre: 15 mins | Cooking: 15 mins

Ingredients:

- 1/4 teaspoon (1.25g) of salt
- 1 pound (450g) of chopped candied cherries
- 1 cup (225g) of margarine or butter
- 1 cup (200g) of caster sugar
- 2 1/2 cups (300g) of plain flour
- 5 eggs
- 1/4 cup (60ml) of red wine
- 8 cups (960g) of chopped pecans
- 1 teaspoon (2.5g) of ground cinnamon

Directions:

1. Sift the cinnamon, flour, and salt into a bowl. Cream the margarine and sugar in a

separate large mixing bowl until light and creamy. 1 cup of the sifted dry ingredients should be added now. To create a batter, whisk together the eggs and wine.

2. Toss the remaining flour mixture with the chopped pecans and candied cherries, then fold in the batter.

3. Bake cookies for 12 to 15 mins in a preheated oven.

Recipe 2. Chocolate Cherry Cookies

Servings: 24 | Pre: 20 mins | Cooking: 15 mins

Ingredients:

- 1/2 cup (50g) cocoa powder
- 1 egg
- 1/2 teaspoon (2.5ml) vanilla extract
- 1 teaspoon (5g) bicarbonate of soda
- 1/2 cup (50g) cocoa powder
- 1 1/2 cups (180g) plain flour
- 1/2 cup (115g) butter
- 1 teaspoon (5g) salt
- 1 cup maraschino cherries
- 3/4 cup (150g) sugar

Directions:

1. Mix in the butter and sugar, then cream them together until they get all fluffy.
2. Now, crack in that egg you've got ready, add some vanilla, and give it a good mix until everything's nicely combined.
3. In a separate bowl, mix together your flour, baking cocoa, baking soda, and a pinch of salt.
4. Take those maraschino cherries, fold 'em into the mix, and then plop spoonfuls of the dough onto your baking sheet. Bake for about 10-15 mins until it's done.

Recipe 3. Chocolate Chip Peppermint Cookies

Servings: 30 | Pre: 20 mins | Cooking: 22 mins

Ingredients:

- 1/2 cup (100g) packed brown sugar
- 1 egg
- 1 1/2 cups (180g) plain flour
- 1 cup (175g) semisweet chocolate chips
- 1/4 teaspoon (1.25g) salt
- 3/4 cup (170g) butter
- 1 teaspoon (5ml) peppermint extract
- 1 teaspoon (5g) baking soda
- 1/2 cup (100g) caster sugar
- 1/4 cup (25g) unsweetened cocoa powder
- 1 teaspoon (5ml) vanilla extract

Directions:

1. Set oven to preheat at 175°C (350°F). Prepare the cookie sheets by greasing them.
2. Cream together the white sugar, brown sugar, and butter in a large bowl till fluffy and light. Beat egg into the mixture, then mix peppermint extracts and vanilla into the mixture. Mix together salt, baking soda, cocoa powder, and flour; mix them into the creamed mixture gradually. Mix the chocolate chips into the mixture. On the prepared cookie sheets, drop rounded spoonfuls of the dough.
3. In the preheated oven, bake for 12 to 15 mins. Let the cookies cool down on cookie sheets for 5 mins, then transfer to a wire rack to cool thoroughly.

Recipe 4. Christmas Ornament Cookies

Servings: 12 | Pre: 20 mins | Cooking: 10 mins

Ingredients:

- 1/2 cup (120g) butter
- 1/2 teaspoon (2.5ml) vanilla extract
- 2 teaspoons (4g) ground cinnamon
- 1/3 cup (80ml) treacle
- 2 cups (240g) sifted icing sugar
- 2 3/4 cups (330g) plain flour
- 1 teaspoon (5g) bicarbonate of soda
- 1 egg

- 1 teaspoon (2g) ground ginger
- 2/3 cup (133g) packed brown sugar
- 1/3 cup (80g) butter
- 2 cups (240g) sifted icing sugar
- 1 tablespoon (15ml) milk
- 1/2 teaspoon (1g) ground nutmeg

Directions:

1. Set oven to a heat of 190°C (375°F) and start preheating.
2. Beat half a cup of butter or margarine. Put in brown sugar and mix. Blend in molasses and egg. Mix together spices, soda and 2-3/4 cups of flour in another bowl. Pour into the beaten mixture. Mix thoroughly.
3. On a prepared surface dusted with flour, roll out dough to a 1/8-inch thickness. Cut dough into shapes of your choice. Bake at 190°C (375°F) for 6 to 8 mins.
4. For the frosting: Beat one-third cup of butter. Slowly pour in half a teaspoon of vanilla, one tablespoon of milk and two cups of sifted confectioners' sugar. Beat until the mixture is smooth. Transfer to a pastry bag fitted with small tip and pipe onto cookies to decorate.

Recipe 5. Christmas Style Swirl Sugar Cookies

Servings: 12 | Pre: 2 hours 30 mins | Cooking: 25 mins

Ingredients:

- 2 sticks (226g) of butter, softened
- ½ teaspoon (2.5g) of salt, for taste
- 1 ¾ cups (350g) of granulated sugar

- 2 large eggs
- 2 teaspoons (10ml) of pure vanilla extract
- 6 cups (720g) of all-purpose flour
- 1 teaspoon (5g) of bicarbonate of soda (baking soda)
- 3 drops of red food coloring
- 3 drops of green food coloring
- Some sprinkles, red, white, and green in color

Directions:

1. The first thing that you will actually want to do is prepare your cookie dough. To do this use a prepared large-sized bowl and add in your soft butter and granulated sugar. Beat with a prepared electric mixer on the highest setting until smooth in consistency. Add in your large eggs and pure vanilla. Beat again until combined.
2. Then add in your flour gradually and your baker's style baking soda. Stir gently until just mixed.
3. Once your down is made divide your dough into 3 different pieces. Place each section into its own large sized bowl. Drop your food coloring into two different bowls and using your hands work the food coloring thoroughly throughout the dough.
4. Wrap each piece of dough in a sheet of plastic wrap. Place into your fridge to actually chill for the next hour.
5. Place a roll of wax paper onto a flat surface. Roll out each ball of dough until it is at least ¼ inch in thickness. Repeat with each of your dough balls. Then place each piece of dough over each other. Trim the edges so the dough is even.

Recipe 6. Christmas Sugar Cookies

Servings: 48 | Pre: 20 mins | Cooking: 12 mins

Ingredients:

- 1 cup (240g) softened butter
- 2 cups (240g) icing sugar
- 1 egg
- 1/4 cup (60ml) sour cream
- 1/4 cup (60ml) honey
- 2 teaspoons (10ml) vanilla extract
- 3-1/2 cups (420g) plain flour
- 1 teaspoon (5g) bicarbonate of soda
- 1 teaspoon (5g) cream of tartar
- 1/2 teaspoon (1.25g) ground mace
- 1/8 teaspoon (0.625g) salt
- White candy coating
- Green paste food coloring

Directions:

1. Mix butter and sugar, add honey an egg and sour cream. Mix dry ingredients; slowly put into the creamed mixture and combine thoroughly.
2. Bake about 8 to 10 mins at 325° or till pale brown. Transfer onto wire racks and let cool. Liquify white coating in a microwavable bowl; mix till smooth. Mix food coloring in; sprinkle on cookies.

Recipe 7. Egg Yolk Painted Christmas Cookies

Servings: 24 | Pre: 55 mins | Cooking: 25 mins

Ingredients:

- 1/2 cup (113g) butter, softened
- 1/2 cup (113g) vegetable shortening
- 1 cup (120g) sifted icing sugar (confectioners' sugar)
- 1 egg
- 1 teaspoon (5ml) vanilla extract
- 2 1/2 cups (300g) plain flour (all-purpose flour)
- 1 teaspoon (5g) salt
- 1 egg yolk
- 1/4 teaspoon (1.25ml) water
- Assorted colors of paste food coloring

Directions:

1. Mix butter and add sugar, Add vanilla and egg; beat well. Mix salt and flour; stir into creamed mixture.
2. Bake for 9 to 10 mins.

Recipe 8. Frosted Reindeer Cookies

Servings: 32 | Pre: 40 mins | Cooking: 26 mins

Ingredients:

- 1 roll Pillsbury® refrigerated sugar cookie dough
- 1/4 cup (30g) plain flour
- 1 cup (240g) vanilla creamy ready-to-spread frosting
- 64 small pretzel twists
- 64 semisweet chocolate chips
- 16 gumdrops, cut in half

Directions:

1. Crumble cookie dough in a big bowl. Knead or mix in the flour to blend thoroughly. Reform to triangle-shaped log. Chill for maximum of half an hour on case very soft to slice into pieces.
2. Preheat the oven to 350 ° F. Slice dough using a sharp, thin knife into 32 triangular pieces about 1/4-inch in size. Arrange the slices on unoiled cookie sheets, spacing 2-inch away.
3. Bake till firm, for 7 to 11 mins. Allow a minute to cool; take out of cookie sheets onto cooling rack. Cool fully for approximately 15 mins.
4. Ice cookies with icing. For the antlers, put 2 pretzel twists on every triangle close the corners. Press 2 chocolate chips lightly in every cookie for eyes and a gumdrop slices in half for nose. Keep among waxed paper sheets in a container with tight cover.

Recipe 9. Holiday Cutout Cookies

Servings: 32 | Pre: 2 hours 45 mins | Cooking: 18 mins

Ingredients:

- 1 2/3 cups (200g) plain flour
- 3/4 cup (90g) wholemeal flour
- 1 teaspoon (5g) baking powder
- 1/4 teaspoon (1.25g) salt
- 1/3 cup (80g) low-fat firm silken tofu
- 1 large egg
- 1 cup (200g) sugar
- 1/4 cup (60ml) rapeseed oil
- 1 tablespoon (15g) butter, softened
- 2 teaspoons (10ml) vanilla extract
- Cinnamon-Sugar Topping, or Decorator Icing (no conversion needed for these)

Directions:

1. In a medium-sized bowl, combine salt, baking powder, whole-wheat flour, and all-purpose flour.
2. Blend tofu into puree in a food processor. Put in vanilla, butter, oil, sugar, and egg; pulse until no lumps remain, stopping and scraping down the sides of the work bowl once or twice. Put in dry ingredients; process until incorporated.
3. Turn dough onto a work surface lightly coated with flour; knead dough several

times. Cut dough into 2 portions; flatten each piece of dough into a disk. Sprinkle flour over the disks; wrap the disks in plastic wrap. Chill dough in the fridge for a minimum of 2 hours or overnight.

4. Set oven to 350°F to preheat. Grease several baking sheets with cooking spray or line them with parchment paper.
5. Roll dough slightly less than 1/4-inch thick on a work surface lightly coated with flour, working with 1 portion at a time. Use a cookie cutter to cut out shapes. Accumulate scraps and re-roll. Arrange cookies approximately 1/2 inch apart on the prepared baking sheets. Sprinkle top with cinnamon-sugar topping (if using).
6. Bake cookies for 12 to 16 mins in the preheated oven, one sheet at a time, until edges turn light golden. Remove cookies to a wire rack and allow to cool thoroughly.
7. Garnish cookies as desired in case you use Decorator Icing. Allow to sit for about 30 to 45 mins or until frosting is hardened.

Recipe 10. Snowflake Sugar Cookies

Servings: 24 | Pre: 50 mins | Cooking: 18 mins

Ingredients:

- 3 cups (360g) flour
- 1/2 teaspoon (2.5g) baking powder

- 1/4 teaspoon (1.25g) salt
- 1 cup (225g) butter, softened
- 1 cup (200g) sugar
- 1 egg
- 2 teaspoons (10ml) lemon extract (optional)
- Coloured sprinkles
- 2 cups (240g) icing sugar
- Milk
- Reynolds® Parchment Paper

Directions:

1. Turn on the oven to a heat of 375°F to preheat. Use Reynolds(R) Parchment Paper to line cookie sheet; set aside. Use an electric mixer to beat together sugar and butter to fluffy. Add lemon extract and egg; beat to well-combined.
2. In a separate bowl, mix together salt, baking powder and flour. Add flour mixture to butter mixture and slowly beat so that it is smooth. Cut the dough into 2 pieces; press into 2 flat disks to shape. Use parchment paper to wrap dough; put into the refrigerator for 1 hour until it is firm enough to roll. Place the dough between 2 sheets of parchment paper that have been lightly floured and roll until it is 1/8-inch thick.
3. Use 2-to-6-inch snowflake cookie cutters to cut the dough. Transfer cookies to cookie sheet lined with parchment paper, 1-inch away from each other. Use colored sprinkles to decorate. Put into the oven to bake until the edges of the cookies begin to brown or for 8-10 mins. Let them cool.
4. In a small-sized bowl, combine milk and powdered sugar; pour milk in slowly to adjust the consistency to your liking. Pour slightly onto the cooled cookies.

Each of the aforementioned cookie recipes has distinct characteristics that contribute to their appeal, giving them a lovely inclusion in your holiday celebrations. Whether one has extensive experience in baking or is embarking on the initiation of a personal tradition of cookie-making, the following recipes have been meticulously crafted to ensure accessibility, delectability, and an abundance of celebratory ambiance.

During the festive period, assemble your cherished individuals in the culinary space, activate traditional Christmas melodies, and commence a culinary undertaking centered on the creation of cookies. The practice is a longstanding custom that not only produces delectable confections but also fosters enduring recollections. Begin by preheating your ovens, assembling the necessary materials, and allowing the pleasurable act of baking to permeate your living space with a sense of comfort and affection.

This festive selection offers a wide range of options, catering to many preferences, from the timeless charm of gingerbread to the contemporary delight of red velvet crinkle cookies. May the process of preparing cookies begin, and may your Christmas season be characterized by affection, mirth, and a plentiful supply of delectable treats.

Conclusion

As you wrap up your exploration of "The Complete Cookie Cookbook," it's time to reflect on your journey, celebrate your achievements, and look ahead to more delightful cookie adventures.

Reflecting on Your Baking Journey

Your ambition to make delicious cookies for family started your cookie-making quest. You know the science behind cookies and their history. You've discovered how to balance ingredients for optimum cookie texture and taste.

Throughout this book, you've explored various dough styles and techniques, stocked your pantry wisely, and discovered the art of creative cookie decoration. Your baking skills have evolved, and you've gained confidence in choosing the right tools and converting measurements accurately.

Keep Exploring and Baking

While this guidebook provides a solid basis, your cookie-baking experience continues. Cookie options are infinite. Keep trying different recipes, tastes, and methods. Share your baking with loved ones to provide pleasure.

Remember that every batch is an opportunity for creativity and discovery. Embrace the process, enjoy the delightful aromas, and savor every bite of your freshly baked cookies.

Happy Baking!

In the end, making cookies is about love and giving. With this cookbook's expertise and recipes, enter the kitchen with confidence, put on your apron, and smell the fresh-baked cookies. Your baking should always offer you joy, warmth, and wonderful memories.

From our kitchen to yours, we wish you endless joy and happy baking!

References:

Images: Freepik.com.

Some images within this book were chosen using resources from Freepik.com

Printed in Great Britain
by Amazon